John McCain

A Little Golden Book® Biography

By Gram Adams
Illustrated by John Joven

Text copyright © 2023 by Gram Adams
Cover art and interior illustrations copyright © 2023 by John Joven
All rights reserved. Published in the United States by Golden Books, an imprint of Random House Children's Books, a division of Penguin Random House LLC, 1745 Broadway, New York, NY 10019. Golden Books, A Golden Book, A Little Golden Book, the G colophon, and the distinctive gold spine are registered trademarks of Penguin Random House LLC.
rhcbooks.com
Educators and librarians, for a variety of teaching tools, visit us at RHTeachersLibrarians.com
Library of Congress Control Number: 2022941306
ISBN 978-0-593-64508-6 (trade) — ISBN 978-0-593-64509-3 (ebook)
Printed in the United States of America
10 9 8 7 6 5 4 3 2 1

John Sidney McCain III was born on August 29, 1936, on a naval air base in Panama. His father and grandfather—also named John McCain— were officers in the United States Navy. John's father was stationed in Panama when his mother, Roberta, gave birth.

Many people in John's family served in the military, dating all the way back to the Revolutionary War. For John, it seemed like he always knew what he would grow up to be.

During John's childhood, World War II was brewing overseas. John's father and grandfather commanded important missions in the war, while his mother took care of the family back home.

Because his father served in the navy, John's family moved often. Changing schools so much made it difficult to learn. But John's mother made sure to teach John and his siblings, Sandy and Joe, as much as she could. Whenever they traveled somewhere new, the family would stop to visit historical places, museums, and natural wonders.

When he visited his grandmother, John liked to read the books his father left behind in his childhood bedroom. He lost himself in adventure novels. For John, the tales of bravery were a reminder to always be true to himself.

John went to a boarding school as a teenager. This allowed him to stay at the same school for years instead of continuing to move from place to place.

John liked his new school. His best subjects were history and literature. His English teacher and football coach, Mr. Ravenel, thought John might make a good leader. When there was an argument among the football team, Mr. Ravenel trusted John to help the players come to an agreement.

Unlike John, the other boys at boarding school came from wealthy families. Most of them knew they would go to expensive universities after graduation. John knew where he would go, too—but it would be very different.

Just as his father and grandfather did before him, John went to the Naval Academy in hopes of becoming an officer in the United States Navy. It was very difficult at first. There were many rules to follow, and John preferred to make his own decisions. He and his friends got in trouble for speaking out of turn, having a messy room, and even sneaking a television into their dorm.

But when it came time to learn how to command a ship at sea, John loved it—and did it well. The ship's captain allowed him to steer, even during difficult moves.

After he graduated from the academy and joined the navy as an officer, John decided to follow in his grandfather's footsteps and become an aviator. He learned to fly planes and lived on huge ships called aircraft carriers.

During these years, the United States was involved in another war, this time in Vietnam. John would head there soon.

In Vietnam, John flew combat missions over enemy territory. After only a few months, his plane was shot down. John survived, but he was captured by the North Vietnamese forces and became a prisoner of war.

John stayed in prison for more than five years. He was often sick, injured, and alone, with little to eat. There were other American prisoners there, too. Even when he couldn't see them, knowing they were there together gave John strength and hope.

By this time, John's father was a very important admiral in the navy. The North Vietnamese thought releasing a famous man's son would make them look good to the rest of the world. But John refused to leave. He insisted that the prisoners should be released in the order they were captured.

That is what happened, but not until the war finally ended. After John got home in 1973, he received many awards for his service and bravery.

After John retired from the navy, he still wanted to serve his country. He decided to run for office. He was elected to the United States House of Representatives and then the Senate, representing the state of Arizona.

As a politician in the Republican Party, John became known as a *maverick* because he made his own choices about how to vote, even if it wasn't what the other members of his party wanted.

After all these years, John was still fiercely independent—and yet he knew from his time in the war that no one is ever alone. He built strong ties with the people in his party and the opposing Democratic Party by working together on shared goals.

His strategy was popular. John was reelected to the Senate five times.

After many years in the Senate, with his wife, Cindy, and seven children by his side, John decided to set out on his next adventure: running for president.
John wanted to win, but he wasn't afraid of losing. He only wanted to run an honest campaign.

In 2000, John lost his party's primary to George W. Bush. In 2008, he ran again. This time he won the primary, but lost the election to Barack Obama. John was disappointed, but he was proud to keep serving in the Senate.

John passed away in 2018. Former presidents Barack Obama and George W. Bush both spoke at his funeral.

Just before his death, the navy rededicated the ship named after John's father and grandfather. The USS *John S. McCain* was now officially named after all three Johns. The ship's motto is "Fortune Favors the Brave."

Thanks to his bravery, John McCain is remembered for making huge sacrifices for his country, for being his own person, and for always looking ahead to the next adventure—just like a true maverick!